Valerie Steele

THE BLACK DRESS

COLLINS DESIGN
An Imprint of HarperCollinsPublishers

First Edition

First published in 2007 by:
Collins Design
An Imprint of HarperCollinsPublishers
10 East 53rd Street
New York, NY 10022
Tel: (212) 207-7000
Fax: (212) 207-7654
collinsdesign@harpercollins.com
www.harpercollins.com

Distributed throughout the world by:
HarperCollins*Publishers*
10 East 53rd Street
New York, NY 10022
Fax: (212) 207-7654

BOOK DESIGN BY SHUBHANI SARKAR

Library of Congress Control Number: 2007926042

ISBN: 978-0-06-120904-8
ISBN-10: 0-06-120904-x

Printed in China
First Printing, 2007

FOR PATRICIA AND FRED

ACKNOWLEDGMENTS

Thanks to all of the designers, artists, and photographers who permitted us to show their work. Special thanks to Fashion Group International. I am also grateful to my editor, Elizabeth Sullivan, and to my husband, John S. Major.

LACK IS A UNIQUELY POWERFUL, MYSTERIOUS, AND SEDUCTIVE
COLOR. THE LITTLE BLACK DRESS ATTRIBUTED TO COCO CHANEL
PLAYS ONLY A VERY SMALL PART IN THE HISTORY OF FASHIONABLE
BLACK. TO UNDERSTAND WHY "THAT SPECIAL BLACK DRESS...
IS BOTH CHIC AND ARMOR," WE NEED TO GO MUCH DEEPER INTO
THE HISTORY AND SYMBOLISM OF BLACK.

"Deep, deep—further than politics, than sex or infantile terrors...
a plunge into the nuclear blackness.... Black runs all through the transcript:
the recurring color black." Among other things, Thomas Pynchon's novel
Gravity's Rainbow is a brilliant meditation on the color black: from Domina
Nocturna in her "black uniform-of-the-night" to a soldier's memory of the
enemy Schwartzkommando, which triggers a sequence of "schwartz-" words:
"Blackwoman, Blackrocket, Blackdream...."

The black of fascism, like the black flag of anarchy, evokes the image
of total destruction. At the same time, black clothing can be perversely erotic.
Long identified as the color of mourning, especially in the West, black has
become the color of elegance and luxury.

Throughout human history, black has been associated with night and,
by extension, death and nothingness. Nor is this simply the result of racism,
since traditional African symbolism makes precisely the same association.
Night *is* black, just as blood is red.

Before the invention of electricity, nights were much darker and more
dangerous than they are today. At night the animals come out, and so do
human predators, like the proverbial thief in the night. In *Les Misérables*, the
persecuted hero Jean Valjean says, "Obscurity is vertiginous.... When the eye
sees black, the spirit sees trouble.... In the night, even the strong feel anxious."

Since antiquity, black has often been associated with evil. The Bible makes
many negative references to black, which is linked to sin, death, evil, the devil,
and mourning. Yet black has also long carried positive, "respectable" connotations
of temperance, humility, and asceticism. Black can be both pious and perverse.

"There is a good black and a bad black," writes Michel Pastoureau, the greatest modern historian of color. In the past, there was a clear distinction between good, brilliant black (in Latin *niger*, from which comes the French, *noir*) and bad, matte black (in Latin *ater*, which was associated with black bile). According to Pastoureau, this distinction still exists in Africa, where shiny black skin is regarded as beautiful, while ashy, matte black is perceived as unhealthy and corpselike. Still, overall, black carries primarily negative connotations.

Le Dictionnaire des Mots et Expressions de Couleur: Le Noir explores how black's symbolic association with the devil and evil have led to expressions such as black magic, black mass, and black Sabbath, while the black of death, misfortune, tragedy, violence, and danger spawned idioms such as black death, black sheep, blackmail, black humor, and film noir. Among gamblers, to wear black is to bring bad luck.

There is the black of melancholy and madness (black bile, black dog) and the black of mystery, secrecy, and the clandestine (black market, blacklist, the black continent). There is also black as a racial marker (black power) and, increasingly, the idea of black as a symbol of luxury and chic (black label).

Yet, despite negative associations, black has always played an important role in the history of fashion. Today's formal black evening attire is a direct descendant of the princely black of the Renaissance. The fashion for black developed in Italy as early as the fourteenth century and spread rapidly from Italy to northern Europe, although it coexisted with an equally fervent love of color. Because black dyes were expensive, only the elite could afford to wear black clothes, whether for mourning, as a symbol of authority or piety, or simply as a fashion statement. As early as 1473—in the Jan de Witte triptych, which depicted an elegant female donor dressed in black with a brilliant scarlet sash—the black dress has been presented as attire for the elite.

Philip the Good, Duke of Burgundy (1396–1467), first wore black when his father was murdered by the French in 1419, but his decision to wear black thereafter seems to have signaled both power and virtue. In a court "famous for its splendor," where most courtiers wore brightly colored clothes, his luxurious black velvet gowns looked "not only serious but elegant," according to John Harvey.

The rise of Spanish black was a pivotal moment in the history of fashionable black clothing. Spanish rulers, such as Emperor Charles V (1500–1558) and his son, Philip II (1527–1598), were known for wearing black clothing almost exclusively, a style that recalled the austere garb of Catholic priests.

When he published *The Courtier* in 1528, Castiglione recommended that Italians follow the Spanish fashion for wearing black because it was grave and sober, rather than garish. The Italian poet Campanelli, who was tortured seven times for defending Galileo against the Inquisition, was less enthusiastic about the symbolism of black:

> Black robes befit our age. Once they were white;
> Next many-hued; now dark as Afric's Moor,
> Night-black, infernal, traitorous, obscure,
> Horrid with ignorance and sick with fright.
> For very shame we shun all colors bright,
> …our souls sunk in the night.

Yet even the enemies of Catholic Spain soon adopted sober black clothing. Indeed, black clothing would prove to be extremely popular in predominantly Protestant countries, such as the Netherlands and England, setting the stage for the rise of black in modern European society. Within sixteenth-century Protestant culture, a clear distinction was drawn between colors that were *honnête* (black, white, gray, brown, and blue) and those that were *not* honest, sober, and discreet (yellow, green, and red). Evidence of this distinction can be seen in the innumerable portraits of Protestant worthies in their sober dark attire. (This was also the beginning of the idea that blue is for boys and pink is for girls.)

In his book *Men in Black*, John Harvey focused on black as a sign of authority in men's clothing. Priests and princes wore black, as did judges and executioners. Harvey's examples range from the Black Prince to Hitler's SS, and from the nineteenth-century poet and dandy Charles Baudelaire to Marlon Brando in a black leather jacket. The book opens with a dialogue from Quentin Tarantino's film *Reservoir Dogs*:

> MR. PINK: Why can't we pick out our own color?
> JOE: I tried that once; it don't work. You get
> four guys fighting over who's gonna be
> Mr. Black.

But what about women? Is there a history of women in black? And if so, what does black signify for them? There is Catherine de Medici, the Renaissance-

era queen of France, widowed in 1559, and thereafter always dressed in black. Sometimes described as the Black Queen, she has often been viewed as "the very incarnation of evil" for her role in the St. Bartholomew's Day Massacre. Although she used the sartorial signs of her widowhood for her own political ends, this did little or nothing to enhance the prestige or power of other widows.

Black was certainly a fashionable color for many European aristocrats, especially in the sixteenth and seventeenth centuries. Visitors to the Château of Chantilly outside Paris can still see a portrait of Gabrielle de Rochechouart, dating from about 1574. She wears a pretty black dress with puffy black-and-white sleeves accented with red. She is clearly not a widow, for this is not a mourning dress. At the time, fashionable aristocratic women sometimes wore striking combinations of color and fabric, such as a dress made of black velvet, together with black, white, and brilliant red satin.

More typical of the sixteenth century was the fashion for dressing all in black, except for an accent of white at collar and cuffs. Both men and women wore black clothing, its sober elegance enlivened by dramatic white ruffs that framed the face. Black could also serve to highlight gold. Veronica Spinola Doria, for example, wears stately Spanish black in a portrait (c. 1606–1607) by Peter Paul Rubens. There is nothing remotely sober about her black velvet dress, lavishly decorated with gold clasps and gold-embroidered sleeves, and topped off with a millstone ruff in pale silvery gray. She wears a red carnation in her hair, and is accompanied by a multicolored parrot.

With the rise of French power in the seventeenth century, the fashion for Spanish black went into decline, except in Spain, where women like the Duchess of Alba continued to wear it. Black remained prestigious among the common people, though, and was incorporated into many types of folk costumes. Black was also stylish in Venice, where it was particularly associated with masquerade attire.

Like other colors, black went in and out of fashion. During the eighteenth century, the vast majority of paintings portray women in light or brightly colored dresses. Aristocratic men also tended to wear colorful clothing—even pink silk suits. Dark colors tended to be associated with poverty or advanced age. Élisabeth Vigée-Lebrun's *Self-Portrait* (1791) is a rare example of a young and fashionable woman in a black dress—all the rarer since dresses of the neoclassical era were usually white.

Gradually, over the course of half a century, an increasing number of men began wearing dark suits in the English style. Long associated with professional men and merchants, dark and sober clothing acquired new prestige through its connection with the sartorial style of the English landed gentry. Soon even Frenchmen who were Anglophiles were adopting black suits, which differed radically, both visually and ideologically, from the colorful clothing of traditional courtiers. But black had multiple meanings. The young rake in William Hogarth's *Marriage A-la-Mode* (c. 1743) wears a jet black velvet suit trimmed in gold lace, evoking the princely black of an earlier era, while his horrified steward wears impoverished but respectable black.

Black became *the* fashionable color for men over the course of the nineteenth century. The reasons for this are complicated but appear to be related to the rise of capitalism and democracy. German sociologist and economist Max Weber's theory that Puritanism spawned capitalism is oversimplified, but it is striking that the capitalist bourgeoisie at the time overwhelmingly chose to dress in ascetic black. This was not poor black, but serious, successful, rich black.

To the extent that the businessman's black suit represented a sartorial equivalent to the work ethic, women had no uniform of professional dignity equivalent to the man's black suit. Although many women worked, they were largely excluded from professions and from large-scale capitalist enterprise. The black dresses worn by governesses and shop girls resembled the self-effacing, respectable black worn by lowly clerks, rather than the rich black of the ruling class. Richard Redgrave's painting *The Governess* (1844) shows a poor but respectable young woman forced to go out to work, perhaps because her own family had died.

At the same time, black carried stylish, even romantic connotations for men and women alike. The devil may be the prince of darkness, but the dandy was "the black prince of elegance." In his youth, Charles Baudelaire dressed in black from head to toe, "like a Titian portrait come to life." Later he wore black because he felt it looked more grave and serious, more appropriate to, as he said, "an age in mourning." For artists, it seemed a philistine and materialistic age, in which black clothing was both a "uniform livery of affliction," said Baudelaire, and a heroic statement of individualism. But black proved attractive to many men, not only artists and poets for whom infernal, satanic, *elegant* black was a

as though carved in old ivory, and her rounded arms, with tiny, slender wrists."
Coming from a puritanical libertine like Leo Tolstoy, this was a clue that his
heroine was a sexual being, soon to be adulterous—and therefore doomed.

Black evening dress was considered sophisticated and seductive,
therefore appropriate for married women—and courtesans. Glamorous black
dresses were definitely not suitable for young unmarried girls. In *The Age of
Innocence*, Edith Wharton's 1920 novel, a character representing old New York
society says disapprovingly of Ellen Olenska: "What can you expect of someone
who was allowed to wear black satin at her coming out?"

In the late nineteenth century, not only black dresses but also black
undergarments were associated with sex. The risqué French periodical *La Vie
Parisienne* (1888) warned readers that men who liked black underwear might
"need to see white skin emerging from a black sheath because white skin
itself hardly arouses [them] anymore"—and women were advised that white
underwear sufficed for the virile man. Black was also perceived as especially
erotic in conjunction with pink. According to Baudelaire, the performer Lola
de Valence shone like *"un bijou rose et noir"* [a pink and black jewel]. If black
is the color of sin, pink has been called the exposed color, one associated with
nakedness, blushing, and intimate parts of the body.

Arthur Rimbaud's poem "Vowels" associated colors with sounds, moving
beyond symbolism to synesthesia: "Black A, white E, red I, green U, blue
O." The poem opens with the unforgettable image: "A. Black, hairy corset of
brilliant flies/ Splurging around cruel stenches/ Gulfs of darkness…" This
highly sexual, feminine, and repulsive image would have been absolutely
unacceptable as a source of inspiration for nineteenth-century fashion, but
it seems to look forward to transgressive twenty-first-century fashion by
designers such as Alexander McQueen.

"Black is anterior to light," writes the French abstract painter Pierre
Soulages. "Before light, the world and things were in the most total obscurity.
With light, colors are born." Is black a color or simply the absence of light?
Black and white things—coal, snow—exist, and throughout much of human
history, black and white were regarded as colors. The triad of black, white,
and red goes back to classical antiquity, when these were the three colors, par
excellence, that represented darkness, light, and bright color.

But in the seventeenth century, when Isaac Newton discovered the
spectrum of colors in the rainbow, black and white were suddenly excluded

from the scientific view of color as light waves of differing lengths. Yet new interpretations of black do not obliterate old ones: Science, myth, and sensory experience can and do coexist in the human mind.

Black has always played an important role in art. Painters from Caravaggio and Rembrandt to Manet and Whistler have made black pigment central to their work. Quite apart from the depiction of men and women in black clothing, which was especially important in the sixteenth, seventeenth, and nineteenth centuries, painters often used black to emphasize the contrast between shadow and light, or to create a sense of volume and mystery. "Le noir est une couleur" ["Black is a color"], insisted Henri Matisse. "Black with ultramarine has the heat of tropical nights; tinged with Prussian blue, the cool of glaciers." For many modern abstract artists—such as Kazimir Malevitch, Aleksandr Rodchenko, Ad Reinhardt, and Mark Rothko—black represented a kind of ultimate end.

The invention of photography in the mid-nineteenth century created a new way of looking at the world—in black and white. Much later, films such as *The Wizard of Oz* (1939) would explicitly contrast visions of the world in black and white and in living color—or at least in Technicolor. *My Fair Lady* also included a striking sequence of black-and-white fashions designed by Cecil Beaton for the Ascot horse race scene, which recalled the black Ascot of 1910 when London society mourned King Edward VII's death.

Around 1910, brilliant colors became highly fashionable in art with the advent of fauvism; in theater, exemplified by Léon Bakst's sets and costumes for the Ballet Russes' *Scheherazade*; and in dress. The couturier Paul Poiret was especially instrumental in promoting bright, "barbaric" colors, such as orange, purple, peacock blue, and lemon yellow. He saw himself as unleashing "a few rough wolves" amongst the sweet pastels then in fashion.

"Scheherazade is easy," sneered Chanel. "A little black dress is difficult." Professing herself to be "nauseated" by Poiret's wild, orientalist colors, she helped inaugurate the reign of neutrals such as beige and black. Many people believe that black was almost exclusively worn as mourning dress until the 1920s when Coco Chanel supposedly "invented" the little black dress. This picture, however, is greatly oversimplified.

In her book *Dressed in Black*, Valerie Mendes suggests, "The 'little black dress' was born some time in the early 1900s, receiving special attention after the death of Edward VII in 1910." Black was certainly recognized as "the garb of

mourning and woe and the emblem of death and destruction." But, again, it was also a fashionable color. During World War I, black was the dominant color in fashion, partly because so many Europeans were in mourning. Throughout the war years, various fashion magazines praised "the many little models in black," such as a "charming little black satin dress."

In 1922, the couture house Premet turned out "a plain boyish-looking little slip of a frock, black satin with white collar and cuffs," which was named La Garçonne after the best-selling novel of the same name. According to *Paris on Parade* (1924), Premet's Garçonne achieved "probably the most sensational success reached by any individual dress model of recent years….Counting both licensed and illegitimate reproduction, a million Garçonnes were sold over the earth." And as Emily Post's famous 1922 *Etiquette* manual reported: "It is tiresome everlastingly to wear black, but nothing is so serviceable, nothing so unrecognizable, nothing looks so well on every occasion."

The popular association of Chanel with the little black dress dates from the October 1, 1926, issue of American *Vogue*, which described a black day dress as "The Chanel 'Ford'—the frock that all the world will wear." Of course, Chanel had designed and worn black dresses before this date, especially following the death of her lover, Arthur "Boy" Capel, in 1919. Although Chanel did not invent the little black dress, her version of the style was extremely influential. Black was a central element in her modernist design philosophy, and she was often photographed in black.

Chanel's greatest competitor, Elsa Schiaparelli, also favored black. According to her autobiography, *Shocking Life*, her clients were "ultrasmart" women who liked "severe suits and plain black dresses." Schiaparelli also recognized that black provided the best background for her witty embroideries.

If black was central to Paris fashion, it was almost equally iconic in Hollywood. The cinema has created indelibly stylish images of movie stars in glamorous black dresses. Marlene Dietrich was especially influential in making black look diabolically elegant. Perhaps most famous for cross-dressing in black tuxedos, Dietrich wore an extraordinary femme fatale wardrobe in *Shanghai Express* (1932), created especially for her by Hollywood costume designer Travis Banton.

Banton also designed some of Anna May Wong's most glamorous costumes for Paramount Pictures. The infamous gleaming black strapless duchesse satin dress worn by Rita Hayworth in *Gilda* (1946) was designed by Jean Louis, who also designed the nude sequin gown Marilyn Monroe wore to serenade President John F. Kennedy in 1962. No wonder Hollywood costumiers spoke of "sexy satin"! Later Hubert de Givenchy's designs for Audrey Hepburn in *Breakfast at Tiffany's* (1961) helped permanently imprint an image of the little black dress the world over. Yet popular attention focused more on Audrey Hepburn herself than on Givenchy, and she was equally striking in slim black trousers and a black sweater. Other couturiers, however, made black central to their own design aesthetic.

Cristóbal Balenciaga, perhaps the greatest couturier of the twentieth century, found black the perfect vehicle for clothing of almost abstract splendor. "Here the black is so black that it hits you like a blow," declared *Harper's Bazaar* (October 1938). "Thick Spanish black, almost velvety, a night without stars." Using stiff fabrics like silk gazar, Balenciaga created clothing that evoked ecclesiastical garments of powerful simplicity. His use of jet black embroideries and magnificent black jewelry also harked back to the golden age of Spain.

The most influential designer of the 1950s, Christian Dior was even more enamored with black. "I have no wish to deprive fashion of the added allure and charm of color, but I could perfectly well design a whole collection simply in black or white," said Dior. "Color cannot transform a failure of a dress into a success; it merely plays a supporting role in the cast where cut is the star performer."

"You can wear black at any time," insisted Dior. "You can wear it at any age. You can wear it on almost any occasion. A 'little black frock' is essential to a woman's wardrobe. I could write a book about black."

Dior was clearly in touch with the zeitgeist, since, as fashion writer Ellen Melinkoff pointed out, "black was *the* basic color" in the 1950s. Oral histories with ordinary American women testify that "black dresses were every woman's answer to the problem of what to wear…. If there were 10 women at a party, nine would be in black." Why this obsession with black clothes? "We felt safe with black. It symbolized sexiness and adulthood. Black on young girls was frowned upon. Our mothers told us we would look like old crones in it and forced us into namby-pamby pastels. *They* (and we also) knew that black had power behind it."

Black is "worldly, elegant, plainly alluring—indispensable," declared British *Vogue* (September 1957). And other fashion authorities agreed. "From 6 P.M. on…is the moment of triumph for the famous 'little black dress,' somewhat décolleté, made of sheer wool or silk crêpe, and with all of its chic concentrated on its line and cut," declared Madame Genevieve Antoine Dariaux, author of *Elegance* (1964).

The dancer Martha Graham, like the Parisian singer Juliet Greco, helped make black equally au courant in avant-garde artistic circles. Beatniks, jazz musicians, and existentialists wore the iconic black of rebels. Black leotards and tights, black turtlenecks and sunglasses, black leather jackets—all created the context within which black would become the most important color in fashion.

By the 1960s, however, black began to fall out of fashion. In an age of youthquake fashions, space-age white and neon brights took center stage. Of course, there were exceptions: Cecil Beaton photographed Twiggy for *Vogue* (April 1967) in Biba's "deep black tragedy" minidress. Fetishistic black also made an appearance in the television show *The Avengers*, with Diana Rigg dressed fierce and sexy in a black leather catsuit. Although best known for his magnificent use of color, the great French designer Yves Saint Laurent helped reintroduce chic black dressing in the 1970s.

But more important than individual designers was the influence of street style in the 1970s. Over the course of that decade, the Empire of Fashion broke up into innumerable style tribes, and subcultural styles exerted an increasingly powerful influence on the world of fashion. Reacting against the love and peace of the hippies, the punks advocated the aesthetics of anarchy and nihilism. Black bondage gear became a punk uniform, along with ripped black fishnet stockings and black underwear worn as outerwear. Vivienne Westwood, herself a punk, was the first designer to be associated with the style. But punk rapidly invaded the entire fashion world.

Goth style was even more focused on black—from neo-Victorian black dresses and corsets to black fingernail polish. The London boutique Symphony of Shadows catered to stylish goths. Once again, designers pillaged subculture, creating goth-inspired fashions and even beauty products, such as Chanel's Vamp nail polish. The combined influence of punk, goth, and "sexy London Soho black" irrevocably altered the significance of black throughout the fashion system, setting the stage for the Japanese fashion revolution of the 1980s.

"Down the catwalk, marching to a rhythmic beat like a race of warrior women, came models wearing ink-black coat dresses," reported Suzy Menkes in 1983. Rei Kawakubo's collections for Comme des Garçons stunned the fashion world. The overwhelming inky blackness of Kawakubo's work initially seemed depressing and ominous to most fashion journalists, who tended to interpret it in terms of mourning and nuclear destruction. Kawakubo herself said that she felt "comfortable" with black and later noted, "I work in three shades of black." Soon anyone, male or female, who wanted to look hip or serious or just stylish was wearing black. As Deyan Sudjic reported in 1986: "[Kawakubo's] clothes are behind the wave of monochrome minimalism that has turned every fashionable gathering in London, New York, Paris, and Tokyo into a solid, all-black wall."

"The samurai spirit is black," said Yohji Yamamoto, another great Japanese designer known for his use of black. "The samurai must be able to throw his body into nothingness, the color and image of which is black." Yamamoto was also known for his partiality to a very dark indigo that verged on black. As he explained, "It wasn't exactly black but an indigo blue dyed so many times it is close to black." Anathematized at first, avant-garde Japanese fashion rapidly became identified with an artistic, intellectual, and/or fashion sensibility. At one point, Yamamoto even had a line of evening clothes called, simply, Noir.

Black fashions were also important for many European designers in the 1980s and 1990s. Azzedine Alaia, Claude Montana, and Thierry Mugler all emphasized the sexual power of black. In particular, they explored the use of black leather, previously associated primarily with fetishistic subcultures. Mugler also pioneered the use of shiny black PVC, creating a style that merged fetish, fashion, and fantasy.

But Gianni Versace was the most influential creator of "the antibourgeois little black dress." With his notorious bondage collection, Versace took the gay "leathersex" look and made it chic. Then he renewed the shock of punk with his famous black safety-pin dress, infamously worn by Elizabeth Hurley at the 1994 London premiere of *Four Weddings and a Funeral.* "Just a boring old punk classic," said Versace to describe a dress that made the front pages and entered fashion history.

As early as the 1970s, Karl Lagerfeld was associated with black fashion. His notorious Soirée Moratoire Noire party was held on October 24, 1977, after the Chloé fashion show. The invitation said in no uncertain terms: "tenue tragique noire absolument obligatoire"—tragic black dress absolutely obligatory. Four thousand people came dressed in black; many, including Claude Montana, in hard-core black leather. But at the House of Chanel, where he has reigned since 1983, Lagerfeld truly came into his own. Chanel might have turned over in her grave at the way he threw out her discreet, modernist

aesthetic in favor of bold postmodernism, but he has moved Chanel into the twenty-first century.

Meanwhile, in America, designers such as Donna Karan focused more on black's practical virtues for the successful working woman. In the mid-1980s Karan's capsule wardrobe of cashmere separates demonstrated that black was both chic and slimming. While Giorgio Armani focused on neutrals such as beige and taupe, Karan helped make black as important for day as it was for evening.

Designers who belong to the High Church of Minimalism naturally gravitate to neutrals, especially black. Perhaps the greatest exemplar of this style in the 1990s was German designer Jil Sander, but many American designers are also advocates of black. Minimalists like Narciso Rodriguez love black because it allows one to see clearly that everything extraneous has been stripped away.

The black-clad legions of the avant-garde also identify with what might be called the ideological connotations of the radical absence of color. As the Belgian designer Ann Demeulemeester once put it, "Who could imagine a poet wearing anything other than black?" One of the most influential designers of recent years, Helmut Lang, created edgy, androgynous styles that made black the color of choice for urban warriors of both sexes.

The sex appeal of black makes it a central focus for many designers. Black lingerie dresses, for example, emphasize the eroticism of the naked body while adding the attraction of concealment. But there are always novel ways to explore the allure of the black dress. For example, by drawing on the perverse allure of sexy Sicilian widows, Domenico Dolce and Stefano Gabbana carved out a new angle on fashionable black.

Viktor & Rolf, the Dutch conceptualists, produced one of the most striking black collections of all time, "Black Hole" (fall/winter, 2001–2002). A meditation on the way black reduces fashion to silhouette, the show created controversy by putting all of the models in black makeup. Although the designers' intention was to abstract the silhouettes, some viewers were reminded unpleasantly of the racist history of white performers in blackface makeup.

Black is the color of "deep space" and "the movement of time," says the American designer Ralph Rucci, whose understated yet dramatic clothes appeal to fashion connoisseurs. Cult designer Isabel Toledo also favors black, especially in the form of Spanish-style black lace.

Fashion's most notorious designers today, John Galliano and Alexander McQueen, excel at black dresses. Like their punk progenitor Vivienne Westwood, they recognize that black is uniquely able to express the charisma of deviance and decadence. While some designers focus on the elegance of black, others see in it the color of destruction and sexual perversion. Black has thus become the color most closely associated with both fashion and antifashion.

In the work of Galliano and McQueen, dramatic, high-fashion black meets rebellious antifashion black, with more than a dash of fetishistic, satanic black. Beauty and horror kiss. Today, every designer who pushes the boundaries of fashion must address the power of black. Although it is impossible to list every designer for whom black is significant, young British designers Zowie Broach and Brian Kirkby of Boudicca deserve special mention for making black central to their warrior aesthetic. Best known for their sharp linear tailoring, which is hard and sexy the way the best uniforms are, they also see something fragile and poetic about what they term "the dark frame around things."

Periodically, fashion journalists suggest that black is now so ubiquitous that it has become obvious, lazy, even boring. Fashionable women pay no attention.

THE BLACK DRESS

W

orldly, elegant, plainly alluring—indispensable.

BRITISH *VOGUE* ON BLACK, SEPTEMBER 1957

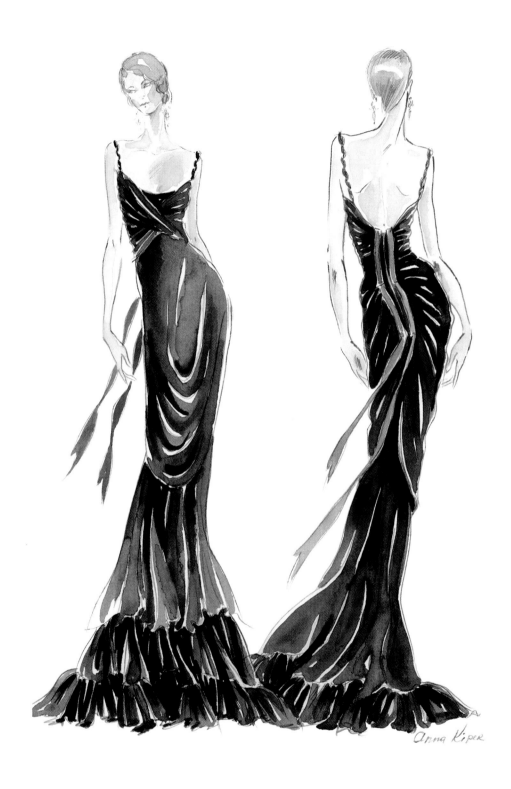

Anna Kiper

To set off to advantage the freshness of a blonde or the fairness of a red-haired woman, it is a soft and deep black that is wanted, the black of velvet. For a brunette, black would be frightfully melancholy…if it were…unenlivened by something glossy, such as Lyons satin or silk.

CHARLES BLANC, *ART IN ORNAMENT AND DRESS*

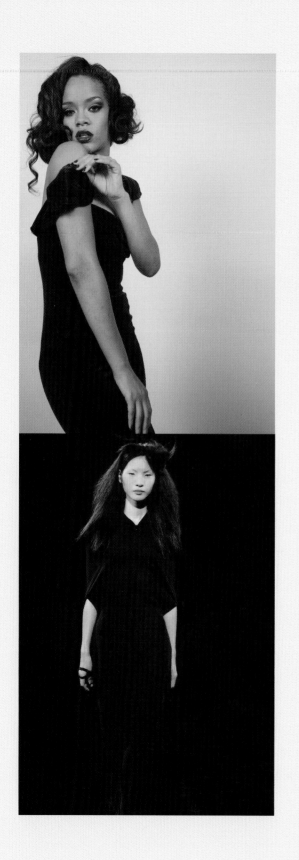

What struck me above all else was the *black*— the absolute black of a little mourning hat. It is a black that could only be Manet's.

PAUL VALÉRY, ON MANET'S *BERTHE MORISOT WITH A BOUQUET OF VIOLETS*

H

ere the black is so black that it hits you like a blow. Thick Spanish black, almost velvety, a night without stars.

HARPER'S BAZAAR, ON THE WORK OF CRISTÓBAL BALENCIAGA, OCTOBER 1938

What can you expect of someone who was allowed to wear black satin at her coming out?

EDITH WHARTON
THE AGE OF INNOCENCE, 1920

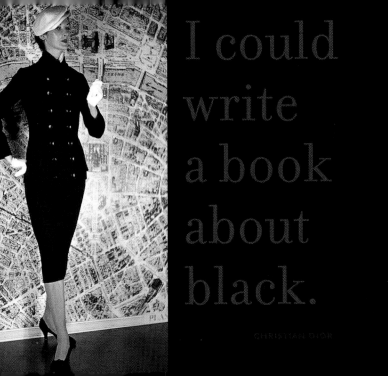

I could write a book about black.

CHRISTIAN DIOR

Tenue tragique noire absolutment obligatoire ("tragic black dress absolutely obligatory").

INVITATION TO KARL LAGERFELD'S 1977 SOIRÉE MORATOIRE NOIRE

THAYAHT. 23

H

ung be the heavens with black!
Yield, day, to night!

WILLIAM SHAKESPEARE, *KING HENRY VI*

Scheherazade is easy. A little black dress is difficult.

COCO CHANEL

I've been forty years discovering that the queen of all colours is black.

PIERRE-AUGUSTE RENOIR

O

bscurity is vertiginous....
When the eye sees black,
the spirit sees trouble....
In the night, even the strong
feel anxious.

VICTOR HUGO, *LES MISÉRABLES*

Deep, deep—further than politics,
than sex or infantile terrors…
a plunge into the nuclear blackness….
Black runs all through the transcript:
the recurring color black.

THOMAS PYNCHON, *GRAVITY'S RAINBOW*

Black **A**,
white E,
red I,
green U,
blue O.

ARTHUR RIMBAUD, "VOWELS"

Divan Japonais

75 rue des Martyrs

Journier
cteur

Hautec

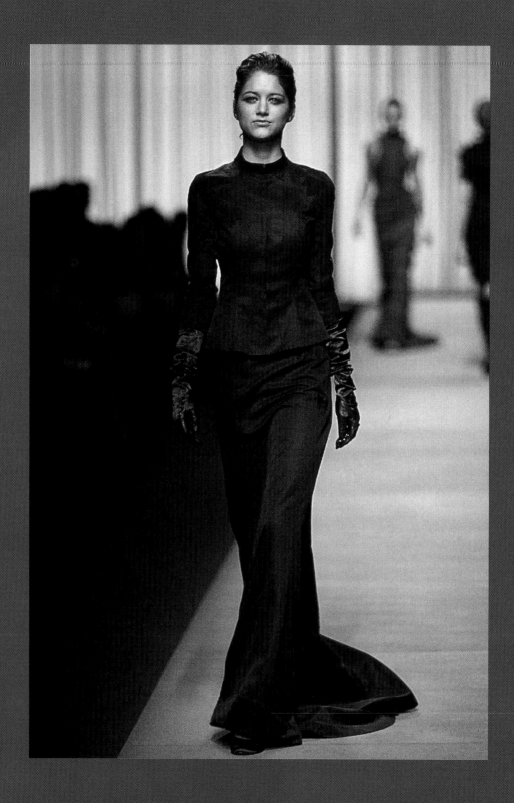

For her fifth wedding, the bride wore black and carried a scotch and soda.

PHYLLIS BATTELLE, JOURNALIST,
ON HEIRESS BARBARA HUTTON'S 1953 MARRIAGE TO PORFIRIO RUBIROSA

The samurai spirit is black. The samurai must be able to throw his body into nothing-ness, the color and image of which is black.

YOHJI YAMAMOTO

J

ust a boring old punk classic.

GIANNI VERSACE, ON HIS SAFETY-PIN DRESS
MADE LEGENDARY BY ELIZABETH HURLEY IN 1994

Any color, as long as it's black.

HENRY FORD

R. Toledo

ILLUSTRATION & PHOTOGRAPHY CREDITS

BIBLIOGRAPHY

ANN DEMEULEMEESTER, BLACK LEATHER DRESS WORN OVER A BLACK SHIRT, FALL/ WINTER 1997. Ann Demeulemeester is known for creating avant-garde clothing which is overwhelmingly black. Her work has a rock-and-roll feel that touches on goth style and is inspired by rebellious individuals such as the singer Patti Smith. As Demeulemeester once said, "Who could imagine a poet in anything but black?" *Photograph courtesy of the Fashion Group International Archives.*

PETER PAUL RUBENS, *PORTRAIT OF VERONICA SPINOLA DORIA*, C. 1606–1607. The practice of wearing black clothing accented with a white ruff at the neck and cuffs was widespread throughout sixteenth- and seventeenth-century Europe. This Spanish-style black velvet dress is lavishly decorated with gold clasps and gold-embroidered sleeves, and topped off with a silvery gray millstone ruff. *Image courtesy of the Staatlichen Kunsthalle Karlsruhe.*

A BETSEY JOHNSON FASHION SHOW AT NEW YORK CITY'S MUDD CLUB, C. 1985. Black dresses are often associated with "bad girls"—an association clearly conveyed by these jailhouse vixens in their micromini dresses deliberately accessorized with trashy fishnet stockings. Here, Betsey Johnson has eschewed the traditional runway show in favor of a sort of performance piece staged at an iconic music venue. *Photograph copyright © Roxanne Lowit.*

ÉLISABETH VIGÉE-LEBRUN, *SELF-PORTRAIT*, 1791. Neoclassical dress was overwhelmingly white, evoking the idea of Greco-Roman statuary. But in this self-portrait, Vigée-Lebrun, the foremost female artist of her time, chose to depict herself wearing a black dress with a flattering white collar that may have alluded to the Flemish fashion for wearing ruffs. Vigée-Lebrun was known for her interest in fashion. *Image courtesy of Il Gabinetto Fotografico, Polo Museale Fiorentino; Uffizi Gallery, Florence, Italy.*

VIKTOR & ROLF, BLACK DRESS STYLED WITH A BLACK MESH FACE MASK, FALL/WINTER 2006. Viktor & Rolf have said that "fashion is more than just clothes; it provides an aura and an escape to reality, a fantasy, a dream." In fashion shows such as "Blue Screen" and "Black Hole," they have used color for fantastic effects. Black face masks, however, proved controversial when journalists thought the look was demeaning to women. *Photograph courtesy of the Fashion Group International Archives.*

RICHARD REDGRAVE, *THE GOVERNESS*, 1844. This wonderful example of Victorian genre painting depicts a poor but respectable young woman who is working as a governess. Unlike her young charges who wear gaily colored clothing, she is dressed in mournful, economical black. Perhaps she has been forced to go out to work as a governess because her own family has died or become impoverished. *Image courtesy of V&A Images; Victoria and Albert Museum, London.*

LEGENDARY MODERN DANCER AND CHOREOGRAPHER MARTHA GRAHAM DANCING IN A BLACK DRESS OF HER OWN DESIGN, 1927 (DETAIL). While classical ballet is aligned with tutus and toe shoes, modern dance became associated with simple black leotards and tights. Modern dancers have also worn costumes like this formfitting black dress, a style that originated among German expressionist dancers. *Photograph by Soichi Sunami; courtesy of Hutton Archive/Getty Images.*

RIDING HABIT, FASHION PLATE BY JULES DAVID FROM *LE MONITEUR DE LA MODE*, 1852. This *costume d'Amazone* was created by Jules Dusautoy, a tailor on the rue Louis le Grand in Paris. Riding habits were traditionally black, based on the model of the man's tailored suit. Here, the tailor has taken the liberty of adding green silk moiré trim. Many arbiters of fashion would have regarded this as an unwelcome novelty, preferring correct, uniform black. *Illustration courtesy of a private collection.*

LE MAÎTRE DE 1473, *TRYPTICH OF JAN DE WITTE* (RIGHT PANEL). Medieval fashion tended to be colorful, although some individuals wore stylish black clothing as early as the fifteenth century. Because black dye was extremely expensive, only the elite could afford to wear black clothes, whether as a sign of mourning, piety, or—as depicted here—sartorial splendor. *Image courtesy of Musées Royaux des Beaux-Arts de Belgique, Bruxelles/ Koninklijke Musea voor Schone Kunsten van België, Brussel.*

"LA MODE NOIR ET BLANC," ILLUSTRATION FOR *FEMINA*, 1910. The contrast between black and white is visually striking, as this fashion illustration shows. The fashions of 1910 tended toward brilliant fauvist colors, such as cherry red, peacock blue, and bright violet. Yet the stylized black-and-white floral print worn by the woman on the right is as eye-catching as a brightly colored ensemble. *Illustration courtesy of a private collection.*

ANNA MAY WONG IN A STILL FROM *LIME-HOUSE BLUES* (1934). The great Chinese-American actress Anna May Wong was featured in a number of Hollywood films. Here she wears a dramatic black evening dress decorated with a gold dragon. Today, this dress, which may have been designed by Hollywood costumier Travis Banton, is in the collection of the Brooklyn Museum. *Photograph courtesy of John Kobal Foundation/Hutton Archive/Getty Images.*

AVA GARDNER WEARS A FORMFITTING BLACK EVENING SHEATH IN THIS PUBLICITY PHOTO-GRAPH FOR *THE KILLERS* (1946). Film noir was a genre perfectly suited to featuring a femme fatale in a knockout black dress. Like hard-boiled crime novels, the film noir featured cynical, weak males and treacherous, deadly females. The diagonal strap bisecting Gardner's creamy bosom is a particularly nice erotic touch. *Photograph courtesy of Photofest Inc.*

GIANNI VERSACE, BLACK LEATHER AND SILK EVENING DRESS, 1992. Gianni Versace was the ultimate creator of what the late Richard Martin once called the "anti-bourgeois little black dress." Versace's use of fetishistic black leather, straps, harnesses, and references to underwear created tremendous controversy. Yet black leather has now been accepted as a legitimate if still ultra sexy material for evening wear. *Photograph courtesy of Maria Chandoha Valentino.*

JEAN PAUL GAULTIER FASHION SHOW, 2006. Models in witchy black dresses parade down the runway for Jean Paul Gaultier, long known as the enfant terrible of French fashion, but today, one of its stalwarts. The picture is striking for the way in which the models' hair—pale blonde and brilliant red—contrasts with the matte black dresses and the surrounding darkness. *Photograph courtesy of the Fashion Group International Archives.*

YOHJI YAMAMOTO, BLACK EVENING DRESS AND "CLOUD" HAT, 1998. Yohji Yamamoto has often collaborated with important contemporary photographers to create unforgettable images of his clothes. This black dress, accented with silvery white sequins, shows how Yamamoto has combined his early interest in asymmetry and the absence of color with an intense exploration of the European couture tradition. *Photograph by Inez van Lamsweerde and Vinoodh Matadin, copyright © Art + Commerce.*

PHOTOGRAPH BY IKÉ UDÉ OF THE SINGER RIHANNA, FIRST PUBLISHED IN *ARUDE*, 2006. The Nigerian-born artist, photographer, and publisher Iké Udé depicts Rihanna wearing a sexy little black dress by Diane von Furstenberg, president of the Council of Fashion Designers of America. At a time when celebrities have become fixtures in the front row, Rihanna created a sensation at New York Fashion Week. *Photograph courtesy of Iké Udé.*

FASHION ILLUSTRATION FROM *ART-GOÛT-BEAUTÉ*, 1925. Although today we associate the little black dress with the work of Coco Chanel, black was central to all fashion designers of the 1920s. This afternoon dress trimmed with white lace, from the House of Doucet, is a good example. Black became extremely fashionable again in the 1950s, but the effect was very different, as the 1920s' Garçonne look gave way to the voluptuous wife-dressing of the 1950s. *Illustration courtesy of a private collection.*

YOHJI YAMAMOTO, BLACK DRESS, SPRING/SUMMER 2001. Throughout his career, Yohji Yamamoto has emphasized the importance of black, sometimes in conjunction with white. He has even had a secondary clothing line called, simply, Noir. By contrast, he has deliberately avoided the sensual and emotional distractions of color, so that on the exceptional occasions when he has used color, it appears doubly striking. *Photograph courtesy of Yohji Yamamoto.*

FASHION ILLUSTRATION BY ANNA KIPER FOR AMERICAN COUTURIER MAGGIE NORRIS, 2006. After many years working for Ralph Lauren, designer Maggie Norris established her own business specializing in custom-made clothes, such as this sensuous black evening dress, which is depicted both front and back by European-born illustrator Anna Kiper. In the past, fashion designers often hired illustrators to document their creations. *Illustration courtesy of Anna Kiper and Maggie Norris.*

GEORGES BARBIER, "LA BELLE DAME SANS MERCI," ILLUSTRATION FOR *LA GAZETTE DU BON TON*, 1921. One of the greatest illustrators of the art deco style, Georges Barbier created this illustration of an evening dress by the House of Worth for the era's most prestigious fashion journal, *La Gazette du Bon Ton*, which presented fashion as art. The name of the dress, "La Belle Dame sans Merci," comes from Swinburne's decadent poem about a cruel and desirable woman. *Illustration courtesy of a private collection.*

EDOUARD MANET, *BERTHE MORISOT WITH A BOUQUET OF VIOLETS*, 1872. Mourning dress looked chic when worn by a young and pretty woman, like Berthe Morisot. Manet was heavily influenced by the use of black in Spanish painting. Camille Pissarro, Paul Valéry, and Stéphane Mallarmé praised Manet's masterful use of black. *Image courtesy of the Réunion des Musées Nationaux de France/Art Resource, NY; Musée d'Orsay, Paris.*

BOUDICCA, BLACK ENSEMBLE, SPRING/ SUMMER 2005. Brian Kirkby and Zowie Broach named their company Boudicca after the Celtic warrior queen who fought the Roman Empire. This ninja-style ensemble from their "Beautiful but Insane" collection was featured in the exhibition *Love and War: The Weaponized Woman* at The Museum at FIT in New York City and demonstrates how the designers use black for dramatic effect. *Photograph courtesy of Boudicca.*

COMME DES GARÇONS, FALL/WINTER 1984. Rei Kawakubo, the designer behind Comme des Garçons, revolutionized fashion in the 1980s by introducing a radically new style of dress: predominantly black, oversized, and asymmetrical. As fashion journalist Suzy Menkes observed, Kawakubo's black-clad models marched down the runway like warrior women. Meanwhile, Donna Karan created practical yet sensual black dresses. *Photograph courtesy of the Fashion Group International Archives.*

CRISTÓBAL BALENCIAGA, 1956. Cristóbal Balenciaga, one of the greatest couturiers of the twentieth century, was based in Paris but often drew on his Spanish heritage for inspiration. Black was the perfect vehicle for clothing of almost abstract splendor. This black lace cocktail dress subtly evokes memories of Francisco de Goya's work and the opera *Carmen*. *Photograph courtesy of the Fashion Group International Archives.*

ALEXANDER McQUEEN, 2003. One of the most important designers to have emerged from the London fashion scene in the 1990s, Alexander McQueen is known for his theatrical runway shows, which feed the popular desire for spectacle. Dramatic sets also enhance the effect of McQueen's structured, highly erotic designs. *Photograph courtesy of the Fashion Group International Archives.*

FRANCISCO DE GOYA, *DUCHESS OF ALBA*, 1799. The rise of Spanish black was a pivotal moment in the history of fashion. Throughout the sixteenth and seventeenth centuries, Spanish aristocrats of both sexes wore sober yet magnificent black attire. Even after black had fallen out of fashion elsewhere in Europe, it continued to play a dominant role in the wardrobe of Spanish women. *Image courtesy of the Hispanic Society of America, New York.*

YOHJI YAMAMOTO, FALL/WINTER 1984. Rei Kawakubo and Yohji Yamamoto are the most important figures in avant-garde Japanese fashion. Both designers showed their collections for the first time in Paris in the early 1980s. Within a few years, they had completely transformed the look of contemporary fashion, and black had become the dominant color in fashion for day and evening. Yamamoto also favored a very dark indigo blue that verged on black. *Photograph courtesy of the Fashion Group International Archives.*

RAF SIMONS FOR JIL SANDER, 2006. Raf Simons recently assumed creative control at the fashion house of Jil Sander, where he explores the possibilities of an elegant minimalism. Designers who work in a minimalist style tend to favor neutral shades. Although Simons has recently shown brightly colored dresses, it is likely that the purity of black dresses like this one will make them especially popular with consumers. *Photograph courtesy of Jil Sander.*

ANN DEMEULEMEESTER, FALL/WINTER 1997. Inspired by the Japanese fashion revolution, Belgian avant-garde designers assumed the mantle of black fashion in the 1990s. Ann Demeulemeester, along with Martin Margiela and Dries van Noten, continues to create advanced fashion. Tough and androgynous, yet oddly poetic, Demeulemeester's clothes are immediately recognizable. *Photograph courtesy of the Fashion Group International Archives.*

JOHN SINGER SARGENT, *PORTRAIT OF MADAME X*, 1884. Virginie Gautreau wears a décolleté black evening dress in this notorious portrait. As originally painted, the dress looked even sexier, because one of the shoulder straps was falling down. The art critic Albert Woolf wrote in *Le Figaro*, "One more struggle and the lady will be free." *Image courtesy of the Metropolitan Museum of Art, Arthur Hoppock Hearn Fund, 1916 (16.53). Photograph copyright © the Metropolitan Museum of Art.*

NICOLAS GHESQUIERE FOR BALENCIAGA, BLACK DRESS, FALL/WINTER 2004. Today, Balenciaga has once again become one of the most fashionable brands under the direction of Nicolas Ghesquiere. For this collection, he utilized a wide range of references, including active sportswear, fashions of the 1980s, graffiti, and even the archives of the House of Balenciaga. The volume of this black dress is artfully controlled by rather startling red chains. *Photograph courtesy of the Fashion Group International Archives.*

CORNEILLE DE LYON [?], *PORTRAIT OF GABRIELLE DE ROCHECHOUART, c. 1574.* Although traditionally associated with mourning, black was also an extremely fashionable color for European aristocrats in the sixteenth century. In this portrait, Gabrielle de Rochechouart is clearly not wearing mourning dress, since her puffy black-and-white sleeves are accented with red. *Image courtesy of Réunion des Musées Nationaux de France/Art Resource, NY; Musée Condé, Chateau de Chantilly.*

GEORGES DE FEURE, ILLUSTRATION FOR *LE JOURNAL DE LA DÉCORATION, c. 1900.* Painter Georges de Feure specialized in "decadent" images of women, such as this art nouveau–style femme fatale. Like the goths of today, the femme fatale was almost invariably depicted wearing elegant, satanic, perversely erotic black. Images of eroticized feminine evil were ubiquitous in fin-de-siècle France, reflecting anxieties about female emancipation. *Illustration courtesy of a private collection.*

HUSSEIN CHALAYAN, BLACK DRESS, FALL/WINTER 2000. One of the most innovative designers working today, Hussein Chalayan frequently explores issues of identity and technology seldom addressed in the world of fashion. This black dress comes from his famous "After Words" collection, which dealt with the plight of refugees. In the most striking sequence from that runway show, chair covers became dresses and a wooden coffee table, a skirt. *Photograph courtesy of Hussein Chalayan.*

RICCARDO TISCI FOR GIVENCHY, FALL/WINTER 2006. Since Hubert de Givenchy's retirement, his fashion house has gone through a number of designers, including John Galliano and Alexander McQueen. Italian designer Riccardo Tisci, best known for a darkly romantic look, is now designing for Givenchy, where his work is often characterized by the use of a theatrical and somewhat gothic black. *Photograph courtesy of the Fashion Group International Archives.*

THAYAHT, ILLUSTRATION OF AN EVENING DRESS BY MADELEINE VIONNET FOR *LA GAZETTE DU BON TON, 1923.* One of the greatest designers of the twentieth century, Madeleine Vionnet pioneered techniques of dressmaking that continue to inspire admiration. This deceptively simple sleeveless black dress is embroidered with an orientalist dragon motif. Thayaht was a futurist artist employed by Vionnet to produce illustrations, which are now collected avidly. *Illustration courtesy of a private collection.*

CHRISTIAN DIOR, BLACK COAT DRESS, FALL/WINTER 1955. "Color can not transform a failure of a dress into a success," said the great French couturier Christian Dior; it "merely plays a supporting role in the cast where cut is the star performer." Throughout his career, Dior emphasized shape and silhouette, creating styles such as the New Look, the H-Line, and the A-Line. *Photograph courtesy of the Fashion Group International Archives.*

AOKI SHOICHI, PHOTOGRAPH OF TOKYO STREET STYLE, 2000. Fashion is not only the preserve of designers and stylists. Individuals, especially young people, also create their own styles—particularly in Japan, where self-fashioning has reached heights of creativity, brilliantly documented by photographer Aoki Shoichi. Inspired in part by his work, legions of photographers now document street style in the world's fashion capitals. *Photograph courtesy of Aoki Shoichi.*

CHRISTIAN DIOR, BLACK SUIT, FALL/WINTER 1954. Dior believed that black was appropriate and flattering for almost all women. Women of the 1950s wholeheartedly agreed, making black the color of choice, especially for cocktail dresses and formal suits. Black was not regarded as appropriate for girls, however, because it carried connotations of sexual sophistication. *Photograph courtesy of the Fashion Group International Archives.*

HELMUT LANG, LASER-CUT BLACK LEATHER, FALL/WINTER 2000. One of the most innovative and influential designers of recent years, Helmut Lang pioneered a synthesis of street style and high fashion, greatly influencing other designers, such as Calvin Klein, who catered to young men and women. This outfit, for example, is street-smart and somewhat androgynous. It is made of fine leather, which has been laser-cut in a pattern inspired by camouflage. *Photograph courtesy of Helmut Lang.*

PRADA, BLACK COAT, FALL/WINTER 2005. Miuccia Prada first made her mark on fashion with her iconic black nylon backpack. A true neophiliac, constantly in search of new looks, she feels no hesitation in making a 180-degree turn from one season to the next. When she loves black, everyone follows suit. Then she will abruptly change and start using deep saturated colors or retro prints. *Photograph courtesy of the Fashion Group International Archives.*

JOHN GALLIANO FOR CHRISTIAN DIOR, CHINESE-INSPIRED BLACK DRESS, FALL/ WINTER 1997. The year that Hong Kong reverted to the People's Republic of China, John Galliano created an entire collection inspired by Chinese fashion. Whereas Yves Saint Laurent had been inspired by fantasies about imperial China, Galliano drew on the iconography associated with Shanghai during the 1930s. *Photograph courtesy of the Fashion Group International Archives.*

YVES SAINT LAURENT, BLACK ENSEMBLE, c. 1980. Perhaps the greatest colorist in fashion history, Yves Saint Laurent was also a master of black, creating looks as iconic as his black see-through blouse and Le Smoking, his famous tuxedo for women. Most designers are lucky if they can create a single signature style, but Saint Laurent was the Picasso of fashion, moving effortlessly from one influential style to another. *Photograph courtesy of the Fashion Group International Archives.*

GABRIELLE "COCO" CHANEL IN A BLACK DRESS OF HER OWN DESIGN, c. 1935. In 1926, *Vogue* featured a black day dress by Chanel, which the magazine described as "The Chanel Ford—the frock that all the world will wear." Of course, Chanel did not invent the little black dress, which was already stylish at the beginning of the twentieth century, but she certainly popularized it. *Photograph by Roger Viollet; Lipnitzki/Getty Images.*

JEAN PAUL GAULTIER FOR HERMÈS, BLACK TRENCH COAT AND TOP HAT, FALL/WINTER 2004. The power of black extends far beyond the little black dress, per se, to include a variety of other black garments and ensembles, such as this equestrian-inspired look for luxury brand Hermès. Just as the nineteenth-century fashion *Amazone* wore a black tailored riding habit, so Gaultier has created a sexy modern equivalent. *Photograph courtesy of Fashion Group International Archives.*

YVES SAINT LAURENT, BLACK DRESS, SPRING/ SUMMER 1982. What Chanel was to fashion design in the first half of the twentieth century, Saint Laurent was to the latter: the single most influential and important designer. Chanel's influence on Saint Laurent is evident in the easy elegance of this little black dress. But Saint Laurent has often been compared with Karl Lagerfeld, who also has an affinity for black. *Photograph courtesy of the Fashion Group International Archives.*

COMME DES GARÇONS, BLACK ENSEMBLE, FALL/WINTER 2004. When Rei Kawakubo first unleashed her black clothes on an unsuspecting fashion world in the 1980s, many journalists and consumers found it depressing, even frightening, and reminiscent of death and destruction. Kawakubo herself recognized that there are many different shades of black, which give different effects. She once said, "Red is black." *Photograph courtesy of Comme des Garçons.*

ALBER ELBAZ FOR LANVIN, BLACK DRESS, FALL/WINTER 2006. Moroccan-born designer Alber Elbaz has brought new attention to the venerable House of Lanvin with his feminine and ever-so-slightly deconstructed dresses. With his fall/winter 2006 collection, he continued to explore the heritage of couture, while bringing it up to date. His pretty party dresses and innovative jewelry received particular acclaim. *Photograph courtesy of the Fashion Group International Archives.*

THIERRY MUGLER, SHINY BLACK DRESS, FALL/ WINTER 1995. The iconography of sexual fetishism is central to Mugler's fashions. His designs often feature tight-laced corsets and kinky boots, and the materials from which his clothes are made tend toward black leather and shiny "wet" black PVC. Black is the fetishist color par excellence because of its cultural associations with sin and evil, and because of the way it contrasts with white skin. *Photograph courtesy of the Fashion Group International Archives.*

PIERRE BALMAIN, BLACK EVENING DRESS, FALL/WINTER 1955. Although never as famous as Dior or Balenciaga, Balmain was a mainstay of French couture during the 1950s, when women believed that black was sophisticated and sexy. Many women especially appreciated the elegant formality of black evening dress: "From 6 P.M. on is the moment of triumph for the little black dress." Later in the evening, the long black evening dress ruled. *Photograph courtesy of the Fashion Group International Archives.*

PIERRE-AUGUSTE RENOIR, *LA LOGE*, 1874. In this painting of an elegant couple in their private box at the theater, Renoir emphasizes the striking effect of black contrasted with white in formal evening attire. During the Middle Ages, striped fabric was known as "the devil's cloth," but the pattern later became highly fashionable. Like Manet and Matisse, Renoir found a special quality in black, which inspired him. *Image courtesy of the Samuel Courtauld Trust, Courtauld Institute of Art Gallery, London.*

FASHION PLATE BY JULES DAVID FROM *LE MONITEUR DE LA MODE*, 1855. The figure on the right wears a fashionable black dress by Mademoiselles Nathalie, dressmakers on Paris's rue de Richelieu. Although the dress closely resembles a mourning dress, the bonnet with pink ribbons establishes clearly that it is stylish day attire. A true mourning ensemble would have had certain prescribed black accessories, such as a mourning bonnet and jet-black jewelry. *Illustration courtesy of a private collection.*

ALEXANDER MCQUEEN, DRESS FROM MCQUEEN'S "BLACK" FASHION SHOW AT EARL'S COURT, LONDON, JUNE 2004. This show and auction included black-themed fashions and works of art donated by celebrities to raise money for Lighthouse Services, an AIDS/HIV charity. McQueen has often emphasized the social and political aspects of his fashions, alluding, for example, to sexual politics and violence against women and homosexuals. *Photograph by Toby Melville, copyright © Toby Melville/Reuters/Corbis.*

AOKI SHOICHI, PHOTOGRAPH OF TOKYO STREET STYLE, 2000. This young Japanese girl has put together a fascinating ensemble—a frilly dark indigo skirt resembling a mini-crinoline paired with a black Vivienne Westwood sweater over a prim white blouse, the look grounded with heavy boots and girlish knee socks. The look is a variant of a style known in Japan as the gothic Lolita, which mixes the gothic black of Victorian mourning with little girl cuteness. *Photograph courtesy of Aoki Shoichi.*

YOSHIKI HISHINUMA, BLACK DRESS, C. 2002. Japanese designer Yoshiki Hishinuma, formerly an apprentice to Issey Miyake, is known for his use of technologically innovative textiles and postproduction treatments, which enable him to create novel shapes and surface effects. This extraordinary dress, with its insectlike silhouette and multiple tones of black, was featured in the 2004 exhibition *Form Follows Fashion* at The Museum at FIT, New York City. *Photograph by Irving Solero, courtesy of The Museum at FIT.*

RALPH RUCCI, BLACK EVENING DRESS, FALL/WINTER 2005. Black is the color of "deep space" and "the movement of time," says Rucci, who studied philosophy and literature before getting a degree in fashion from the Fashion Institute of Technology. Rucci has an affinity for neutral colors, but Halston taught him that super-rich women love color. *Photograph by Dan Lecca, courtesy of Ralph Rucci.*

MARLENE DIETRICH IN AN EXOTIC BLACK ENSEMBLE BY HOLLYWOOD COSTUMIER TRAVIS BANTON IN *SHANGHAI EXPRESS* (1932). Veiled, surrounded by feathers, and adorned with glittering jewelry, Dietrich seems the ultimate woman of mystery: infinitely desirable, but also dangerous, decadent, and deviant. *Photograph courtesy of Movie Star News.*

PHOTOGRAPH BY STEPHAN WÜRTH OF A BLACK ENSEMBLE BY BOUDICCA, *SURFACE* MAGAZINE, 2006. Designers Brian Kirkby and Zowie Broach of Boudicca understand the power of black. Best known for their sharp linear tailoring, which is hard and sexy the way the best uniforms are, they also see something fragile and poetic about what they call "the dark frame around things." *Photograph courtesy of Stephan Würth.*

VIKTOR & ROLF, DRESS FROM THE "BLACK HOLE" COLLECTION, FALL/WINTER 2001. "We were inspired by black holes, which absorb all light and energy," explained Rolf. "We wanted to transform negative feelings into something positive and creative." But some reviewers found the models' makeup uncomfortably reminiscent of "blackface" performers. *Photograph courtesy of the Fashion Group International Archives.*

BLACK DRESS AND CAPE BY ALIX (MADAME GRÈS), 1934. The period between the two world wars was dominated by great women designers including Mademoiselle Alix. Born Germaine Krebs, Alix was ultimately known as Madame Grès. Only two of these women—Chanel and Grès—continued to flourish after World War II, when the fashion world became dominated by men like Dior and Balenciaga. *Photograph courtesy of the Harvard Theater Collection.*

MARC JACOBS FOR LOUIS VUITTON, BLACK ENSEMBLE, FALL/WINTER 2005. Every season, after showing his own collection in New York, Marc Jacobs flies to Paris to show the collection he designs for Louis Vuitton. In 2005, drawing heavily on Japanese avant-garde fashions, Jacobs emphasized black, voluminous shapes in both collections. *Photograph courtesy of the Fashion Group International Archives.*

"AN AMERICAN WOMAN IN A BLACK TAILORED SUIT," ACCOMPANIED BY A BORZOI, C. 1905. The tailored suit was the quintessential modern female fashion at the turn of the twentieth century. Based on the man's business suit and the upper class riding habit, the tailored suit eschewed feminine frills in favor of impeccable tailoring. A masculine palette of dark colors was preferred. Black, in particular, evoked the minimalist aesthetic of the dandy. *Illustration courtesy of a private collection.*

DOLCE & GABBANA, BLACK DRESS, FALL/WINTER 1988. Domenico Dolce and Stefano Gabbana founded Dolce & Gabbana in 1985. Together, they have created a Mediterranean style that draws its inspiration from southern Italian culture. The black-clad Sicilian woman was an important early inspiration for them, especially as seen through the lens of Italian realist films. *Photograph courtesy of the Fashion Group International Archives.*

DAVID LEVINTHAL, "SOLO IN THE SPOTLIGHT," 1998. The most famous fashion doll in history, Barbie first appeared in 1959. During the first decade of her existence, she had many high-fashion ensembles, such as the Black Magic cocktail dress, and the glittering black evening gown, Solo in the Spotlight. Many artists have been inspired by Barbie, but in David Levinthal she finally has found a photographer able to do her justice. *Photograph courtesy of David Levinthal.*

HENRI DE TOULOUSE-LAUTREC, *LE DIVAN JAPONAISE*, 1893. Known as "La Mélinite" (the Explosive), Jane Avril was famous for her performances at the Moulin Rouge. Even seated and covered from neck to ankle, every line of her slender, sinuous figure is revealed by her perversely erotic dress. *Image courtesy of the Los Angeles County Museum, gift of Mr. and Mrs. Billy Wilder.*

DONATELLA VERSACE, BLACK EVENING DRESS, FALL/WINTER 2005. After the death of her brother, Gianni Versace, Donatella Versace continued his signature style of flamboyant sexuality. But Donatella has also successfully embraced red carpet dressing, which draws on the prototype goddess dresses of 1930s' film stars. Whereas actresses like Jean Harlow wore white, today's stars are more likely to wear black. *Photograph courtesy of the Fashion Group International Archives.*

OLIVIER THEYSKENS FOR ROCHAS, BLACK EVENING GOWN, FALL/WINTER 2005. As designer for Rochas, Olivier Theyskens created a number of extraordinary black dresses inspired by the fashions of the High Victorian era. When Rochas closed their fashion department, Theyskens was left unemployed for about a minute before being picked up by Nina Ricci, for whom he created a first collection as light and ethereal as the company's signature L'Air du Temps perfume. *Photograph courtesy of the Fashion Group International Archives.*

NO GLOVE, NO LOVE (DETAIL), 1998. A giant "safe sex" billboard occupying the entire wall of a building along New York City's Lexington Avenue promoted the use of condoms with an image of a voluptuous, latex-clad female body. Naturally, the dress had to be black if it were to convey the look of extreme sexual allure. At a time when AIDS and other sexually transmitted diseases threatened bodily integrity, shiny "wet-look" rubber began to enter the fashion mainstream. *Photograph courtesy of John S. Major.*

DINNER DRESS BY BIANCHINI, ILLUSTRATION BY DILLON FOR *LA GRANDE DAME*, 1894. Black carried ambiguous connotations in the nineteenth century. Although it could "look very economical," it could also be very expensive. Indeed, many fashion writers agreed that the most elegant and flattering dress was likely to be black. *Illustration courtesy of a private collection.*

KARL LAGERFELD FOR CHANEL, BLACK EVENING DRESS WITH GOLD CHAIN, FALL/WINTER 1985. After he took creative control at Chanel, Lagerfeld made the brand successful by constantly updating stylistic signatures such as the double interlocked Cs, the quilting, gold chains, the Chanel jacket, the Chanel pump, and, of course, the little black dress. Today, Chanel is invariably listed as one of the world's top five luxury brands. *Photograph courtesy of the Fashion Group International Archives.*

ISABEL TOLEDO, BLACK LACE DRESS, C. 2005. Isabel Toledo has been described as a designer's designer. Although little known by the general public, she long ago attained cult status among the fashion cognoscenti for her individual sense of style. Born in Cuba, she moved to the United States as a child. Her use of black lace in this dress alludes to a Latin aesthetic. she is now the creative director for Anne Klein. *Photograph courtesy of William Palmer.*

GIANNI VERSACE, SAFETY-PIN DRESS, SPRING/SUMMER 1994. Versace's notorious safety-pin dress is a perfect example of his ability to appropriate subcultural styles that evoke the charisma of deviance. Almost two decades after the heyday of punk rock, safety pins were no longer transgressive symbols of destruction and nihilism, but, as Versace said, "just a boring old punk classic." *Photograph courtesy of the Fashion Group International Archives.*

THIERRY MUGLER, BLACK LEATHER CORSET DRESS, FALL/WINTER 1995. For decades the fashion world's most dedicated exponent of fetish fashion, Thierry Mugler has been drawn to black for its perverse erotic allure. This extraordinary hand-tooled leather ensemble presents the tightly laced corset as the centerpiece of a fantasy costume based on the image of the dominatrix. The black neck corset also serves, visually, to sever the wearer's head. *Photograph courtesy of the Fashion Group International Archives.*

RITA HAYWORTH IN A BLACK SHEATH DRESS BY JEAN LOUIS IN A STILL FROM *GILDA* (1946). Hollywood costumers referred to the shiny material as "sexy satin" because of the way it reflected the light along the body's curves—in this case, some of Hollywood's most famous ones. Jean Louis also created the nude sequin gown that Marilyn Monroe wore to serenade President John F. Kennedy on his forty-fifth birthday. *Photograph courtesy of Photofest Inc.*

YOHJI YAMAMOTO, BLACK DRESS, FALL/WINTER 1997. Within Japanese culture, black is associated not only with the samurai but also with the rustic clothing of the peasantry. Eschewing stereotypes about sexy black dresses, Yohji Yamamoto uses black instead for its abstract, androgynous power. As utilized in his work, black conveys associations of an artistic and intellectual nature. *Photograph courtesy of the Fashion Group International Archives.*

RUBEN TOLEDO, "THREE BLACK DRESSES," C. 2006. With the rise of fashion photography in the 1930s, fashion illustration became increasingly rare. But recent years have seen a revival of the genre, and the leading practitioner is undoubtedly Ruben Toledo. The Cuban-born artist, sculptor, and illustrator has also begun making films, which exhibit his characteristic style of surreal wit and charm. *Illustration courtesy of Ruben Toledo.*

YEOHLEE TENG, CATENARY HARNESS DRESS, FALL/WINTER 2006. Yeohlee has described her clothes as "intimate architecture," and her clothing designs have been featured in exhibitions such as *Skin and Bones: Parallel Practices in Fashion and Architecture* at the Museum of Contemporary Art in Los Angeles. As befits the creator of functional, somewhat austere clothes, Yeohlee's color palette tends toward neutrals suitable for the urban nomad. *Photograph courtesy of Yeohlee.*

AUDREY HEPBURN WEARING A BLACK DRESS BY GIVENCHY IN A PUBLICITY PHOTOGRAPH FOR *BREAKFAST AT TIFFANY'S* (1961). The favorite muse of French couturier Hubert de Givenchy, Audrey Hepburn wore his clothes both on and off screen. Her gamine beauty brought a special charm to the sophisticated luxury of haute couture, but she was equally appealing in simple black trousers and a black turtleneck. *Photograph courtesy of Photofest Inc.*

ISABEL TOLEDO, JERSEY DRESS, C. 2004. Isabel Toledo's look is characterized by fluid, organic forms, often the result of her innovations in pattern-making and construction. This dress is typical of the way she creates a three-dimensional design of sophisticated simplicity. Black and shades of gray dominate her palette in accordance with the abstract quality of her work. *Photograph courtesy of William Palmer.*

RUBEN TOLEDO, "WOMAN WEARING A LITTLE BLACK DRESS AND CARRYING A TIFFANY'S SHOPPING BAG," C. 2006. Best known for his surreal fashion illustrations, which are published in prestigious periodicals such as *Visionaire* and *Vogue*, Ruben Toledo has also created a wide range of commercial images for luxury stores such as Neiman Marcus and Tiffany's. Friends and acquaintances know that he sketches constantly; his muse and model is always his wife Isabel. *Illustration courtesy of Ruben Toledo.*

Armstrong, Carol. *Manet Manette*. New Haven and London: Yale University Press, 2002.

Black Book: Art and Fashion. Paris: Assouline, 1989.

Blanc, Charles. *Art in Ornament and Dress*. London: Chapman and Hall, 1877.

Dariaux, Genevieve Antoine. *Elegance*. Garden City, N.Y.: Doubleday & Co., 1964.

Dior, Christian. *Dior by Dior*. New York: E. P. Dutton & Co., 1957.

Ecob, Helen Gilbert. *The Well-Dressed Woman: A Study in the Practical Applications to the Art of Dress of the Laws of Health, Art, and Morals*. New York: Fowler & Wells, 1893.

Edelman, Amy Holman. *The Little Black Dress*. New York: Simon & Schuster, 1997.

Femmes fin de Siècle, 1885–1895. Paris: Musée de la Mode et du Costume, 1990.

Frieda, Leonie. *Catherine de Medici: Renaissance Queen of France*. New York: HarperCollinsPublishers, 2003.

Harvey, John. *Men in Black*. Chicago: The University of Chicago Press, 1995.

Hollander, Anne. *Seeing Through Clothes*. New York: Viking Press, 1978.

Koren, Leonard. *New Fashion Japan*. Tokyo and New York: Kodansha, 1984.

Lamaire, Gérard-Georges. *Le Noir*. Paris: Hazan, 2006.

Martin, Richard. "Gianni Versace's Anti-Bourgeois Little Black Dress," *Fashion Theory: The Journal of Dress, Body & Culture*. Volume 2, Issue 1 (1998).

Melinkoff, Ellen. *What We Wore*. New York: Quill, 1984.

Mendes, Valerie. *Dressed in Black*. London and New York: V&A Publications in association with Harry N. Abrams, 1999.

Mollard-Desfour, Anne. *Le Dictionnaire des Mots et Expressions de Couleur: Le Noir*. Paris: CNRS Editions, 2005.

Pastoureau, Michel, and Dominique Simonnet. *Le Petit Livre des Couleurs*. Paris: Éditions du Panama, 2005.

Pynchon, Thomas. *Gravity's Rainbow*. New York: Viking Press, 1973.

Steele, Valerie. *Paris Fashion: A Cultural History*. New York: Oxford University Press, 1988; revised edition, Oxford: Berg, 1998.

_____. *Women of Fashion*. New York: Rizzoli International, 1991.

_____. *Fetish: Fashion, Sex & Power*. New York: Oxford University Press, 1996.

Uhlirova, Marketa. "Interview with Zowie Broach and Brian Kirkby of Boudicca," *Fashion Theory: The Journal of Dress, Body & Culture*. Volume 10, Issue 4 (2006).

Wilson, Robert Forrest. *Paris on Parade*. Indianapolis: The Bobbs-Merrill Company, 1924.

Wullschlager, Jackie. "Black's Enigmatic Versatility," *Financial Times*, September 16–17, 2006.